a gift for

_____

from

_____

FAMILIES

with love

L.F.F. GROUP

Other things may change us,
but we start and end with family.

[ANTHONY BRANDT]

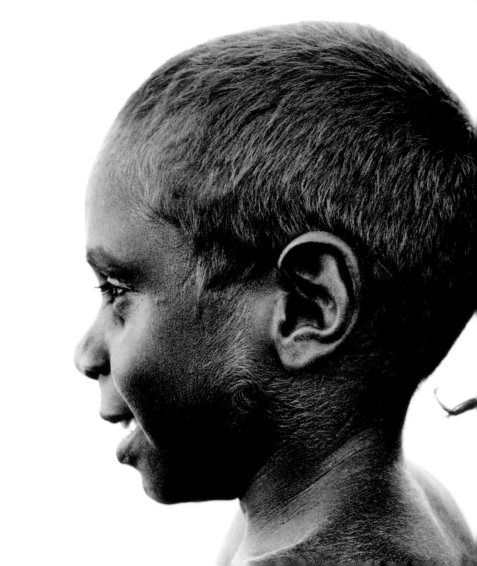

Without the human
community,
one single human being
cannot survive.

[DALAI LAMA]

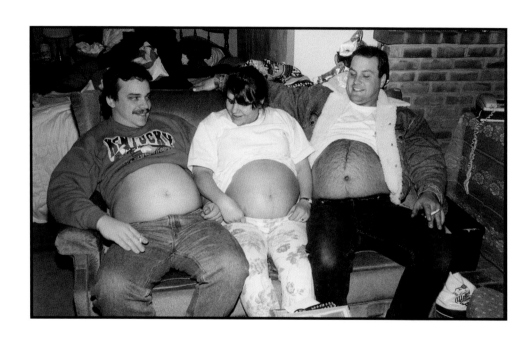

It is the absurdity of family life, the raggedness of it, . . .

that is at once its redemption and its true nobility.

[JAMES MCBRIDE]

Seek the **wisdom** of the ages, but look at the world through the eyes of a child.

[RON WILD]

Children's faces looking up,
holding wonder
like a cup.

[SARA TEASDALE]

So sweet and precious is family life . . .

[JAMES MCBRIDE]

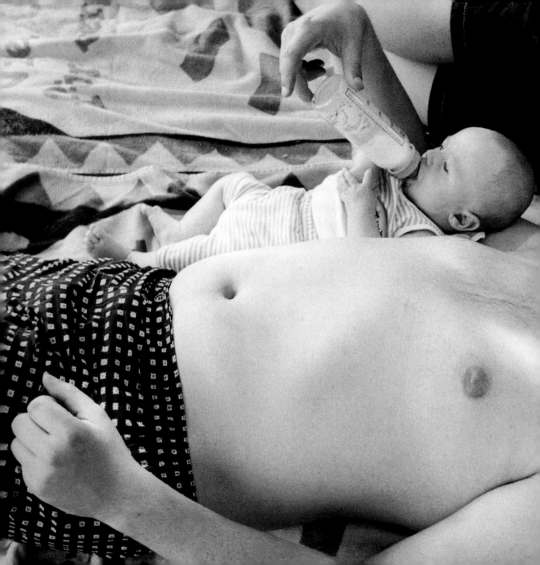

I live for those who love me,
for those who know me true.

[GEORGE LINNAEUS BANKS]

Family faces are magic mirrors.

[GAIL LUMET BUCKLEY]

To have joy one must share it.
Happiness was born a twin.

[LORD BYRON]

Having a place to go –
is a home.

Having someone to love –
is a family.

[DONNA HEDGES]

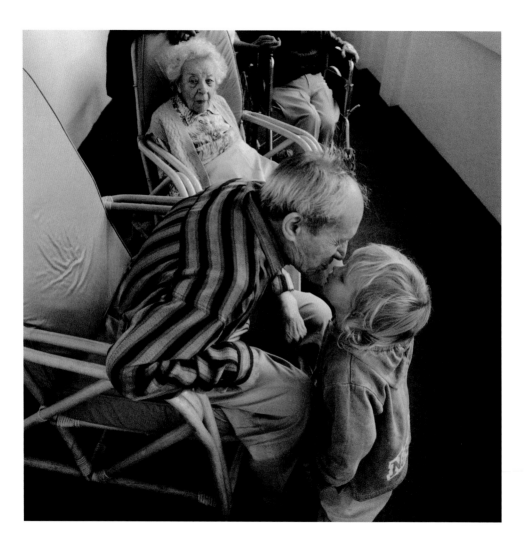

The family – that dear octopus from whose tentacles we never quite escape, nor in our innermost hearts quite wish to.

[DOROTHY GLADYS SMITH]

The family is one of nature's masterpieces.

[GEORGE SANTAYANA]

Family is the last and greatest
discovery . . . It is our last miracle.

[JAMES MCBRIDE]

Page 2
© Roberto Colacioppo, Italy
A great-grandmother's heartfelt embrace of a young bride. The old lady, 97, and her great-granddaughter are the only family members who still live in the mountain village of Roccaspinalveti, Italy.

Pages 4
© Stephen Hathaway, UK
Charles and his grandson Richard are deep in conversation as they sit in Soho Square, London, England.

Page 6–7
© Steven Siewert, Australia
An Aboriginal brother and sister can't hold back the smiles as their photograph is taken in Queensland, Australia.

Pages 8–9
© Joan Sullivan, Canada
The babysitter – in the foothills of the Himalayas, a Nepalese grandfather looks after his two grandchildren while he catches up on news brought from Katmandu by a young porter.

Pages 10–11
© Rachel Pfotenhauer, USA
Circles of celebration – surrounded by their family, Jean and Paul celebrate their 50th wedding anniversary at Lake Tahoe, California, USA. Reunited for this special occasion, their children and grandchildren dance in circles around the delighted couple.

Page 12
© Melonie Bennett, USA
Family likeness – brothers-in-law Jim and Scott compare themselves to nine-months' pregnant Mary, at home in Gorham, Maine, USA.

Page 13
© Michael Agelopas, USA
On the island of Chios in Greece, five sisters share a village bench. By chance or by habit, they sit in chronological order.

Pages 14–15
© Dmitri Korobeinikov, Russia
In the Russian village of Gimenej, heavy rain turns the road to mud on a couple's wedding day. The bridegroom helps to push the car as his bride seeks sanctuary from the weather.

Pages 16
© Guus Rijven, The Netherlands
Overcoming the generation gap in Brummen, the Netherlands. Eighty-one years separate a grandfather from his only grandchild, but that's no barrier to play. Two-year-old Jarón chooses the game.

Pages 18–19
© Sefton Samuels, UK
During a family photo session in Altrincham, Cheshire, England, one-year-old Philip looks unimpressed by the behavior of his older sister, Alice.

Pages 20–21
© Martin Rosenthal, Argentina
A father and his children in Juanchaco, Colombia.

Pages 22–23
© Abu Taher Khokon, Bangladesh
Afternoon sleep in Khulna, Bangladesh – while a family takes a rest in the hot sultry summer, only the mother stays awake.

Pages 24–25
© Lorenz Kienzle, Germany
A family lies in relaxed contentment on the shore of the River Elbe in Germany. While his parents sleep off their picnic lunch, three-month-old Jan enjoys a drink of his own.

Page 26
© Devang Prajapati, India
In the town of Ahmedabad, India, one-year-old Forum is fascinated by the face of elderly neighbor Mrs Champaben.

Page 27
© Katharina Brinckmeier, The Netherlands
The special relationship between two-year-old Myra and her grandmother Mutti, 92, who live in the village of Rautheim in Braunschweig, Germany.

Pages 28–29
© Edmond Terakopian, UK
British Royal Air Force sergeant John has just returned from the Gulf War to his wife, Sharon, and their two-year-old son, Phillip. Their reunion was captured during a press conference in Stanmore, Middlesex, England.

Pages 30–31
© Sayyed Nayyer Reza, Pakistan
Love and kindness bridge the generation gap in Lahore, Pakistan. Nine-year-old Suman shares a playful moment with her elderly friend and neighbor – the old lady is known simply as Amman, an Urdu word for "mother."

Pages 32–33 and back cover
© Mikhail Evstafiev, Russia
On the streets of Santiago de Cuba, Cuba – a couple's uninhibited display of affection raises a spontaneous smile from their young audience.

Page 35
© **Lyn Dowling, Australia**
"Ma" and me – Rebecca, aged 20 months, and her grandmother "Ma" share the simple pleasures of a street festival in Brisbane, Australia.

Page 36
© **Ray Peek, Australia**
Another generation learns about mustering from the head of the family. "Big" Morrie Dingle, a grazier in South Queensland, Australia, and his two grandsons take a break from the saddle to enjoy some food.

Page 37
© **David Williams, UK**
Face to face – in Newcastle, England, godfather David meets his one-month-old godson, Samuel, for the first time.

Pages 38–39
© **Christopher Smith, USA**
Age is no barrier to enjoying a dance at a wedding party in North Carolina, USA. New bride Pamela teaches Uncle Mac the steps, while the bride's parents show how it should be done.

Page 40
© **James Fassinger, USA**
Mirror image – identical twins take a springtime stroll along the banks of the Vltava River in Prague, Czech Republic.

Page 42
© **Christel Dhuit, New Zealand**
They may be twins, but their reactions are very different. Five-month-old sisters in Auckland, New Zealand.

Page 43
© **Philip Kuruvita, Australia**
A woodshed in Tasmania, Australia, provides an unusual playground for identical twins, Summer and Melody.

Page 45
© **Jerry Koontz, USA**
Liaza, aged 12, and her younger sister Adriana, six, at play on the streets of Ajijic village in Mexico.

Page 46
© **Lambro (Tsiliyiannis), South Africa**
Two-year-old Robert greets his 85-year-old grandfather, Christy, in Cape Town, South Africa.

Page 47
© **Paul Carter, USA**
A gentle smile from mother to son in Eugene, Oregon, USA. Nano, 85, suffers from arthritis but is cared for at home by her son, Doug. After an afternoon reading to his mother, Doug lifts her carefully back to bed.

Page 48
© **Ben Law-Viljoen, USA**
Sixty years on – Fransiena, 84, holds a bunch of wild mustard flowers picked for her by Willem, 93. The couple are celebrating over six decades of marriage and stand outside the home they share in Haarlem, South Africa.

Page 49 and front cover
© **Slim Labidi, France**
One-month-old Malik is the center of attention for his loving parents, Cecile and Hafid, photographed at their home in Villeurbaine, France.

Page 51
© **Luca Trovato, USA**
The Gobi Desert, Mongolia – stranded with all their belongings, a nomadic family are relaxed as they await help.

Pages 52–53
© **Chirasak Tolertmongkol, Thailand**
The sun sets over a hill tribe village in Chiang Rai, northern Thailand. While the parents gather in the middle of the village, their children use the main thoroughfare as their playground.

Pages 54–55
© **Herman Krieger, USA**
Surrounded by pictures of her loved ones, 92-year-old Frances reminisces on family life at her home in Oregon, USA.

Page 57
© **Heather Pillar, Taiwan**
Rob Schwartz with his father, Morrie. Mitch Albom, a writer and former student of Morrie, noticed Morrie on a television show and renewed contact with his old professor. The outcome was Albom's moving bestseller *Tuesdays with Morrie*, based on time spent with Morrie on the last 14 Tuesdays of his life.

Pages 58–59
© **Andrei Jewell, New Zealand**
The beautiful mountain scenery of Zanskar in the Indian Himalayas is the setting for a twilight stroll. In a region which is snow-covered for most of the year, Norbu and his young granddaughter make the most of the warm sunshine.

Page 61
© **Thanh Long, Vietnam**
In Phan Rang city, Vietnam, new life is nurtured by age-old experience as this 86-year-old grandmother shares a tender moment with her grandson.

Inspired by the 1950s landmark photographic exhibition, *"The Family of Man,"* M.I.L.K. began as an epic global search to develop a collection of extraordinary and geographically diverse images portraying humanity's Moments of Intimacy, Laughter and Kinship (M.I.L.K.). This search took the form of a photographic competition – probably the biggest, and almost certainly the most ambitious of its kind ever to be conducted. With a world-record prize pool, and renowned Magnum photographer Elliott Erwitt as Chief Judge, the M.I.L.K. competition attracted 17,000 photographers from 164 countries. Three hundred winning images were chosen from the over 40,000 photographs submitted to form the basis of the M.I.L.K. Collection.

The winning photographs were first published as three books titled *Family*, *Friendship* and *Love* in early 2001, and are now featured in a range of products worldwide, in eight languages in more than 20 countries. The M.I.L.K. Collection also forms the basis of an international travelling exhibition.

The M.I.L.K. Collection portrays unforgettable images of human life, from its first fragile moments to its last. They tell us that the rich bond that exists between families and friends is universal. Representing many diverse cultures, the compelling and powerful photographs convey feelings experienced by people around the globe. Transcending borders, the M.I.L.K. imagery reaches across continents to celebrate and reveal the heart of humanity.

www.milkphotos.com

© 2002 M.I.L.K. Publishing Limited, Studio 3.11, Axis Building, 1 Cleveland Road, Parnell, Auckland, New Zealand. Published under license from M.I.L.K. Licensing Limited.

All copyrights of the photographic images are owned by the individual photographers who have granted M.I.L.K. Licensing Limited the right to use them.

First published in Estonia in 2003 by
L.F.F. Group, J.Vilmsi 47-33, Tallinn 10126, Estonia.
www.lffgroup.com

All rights reserved. No part of this publication may be reproduced (except brief passages for the purpose of review), stored in a retrieval system or transmitted in any form by any means, electronic, mechanical, photocopying, recording or otherwise, without the prior written permission of the publisher.

Concept designed by Kylie Nicholls. This edition designed by Holly Stevens. Printed by Midas Printing Limited, Hong Kong. Back cover quotation by George Santayana.

ISBN 0 7336 1702 6

MOMENTS   INTIMACY   LAUGHTER   KINSHIP